D0835467

THE PROBLEM OF
CHRIST IN THE
TWENTIETH
CENTURY

THE PROBLEM OF
CHRIST IN THE TWENTIETH CENTURY

*AN ESSAY ON THE
INCARNATION*

THE MAURICE LECTURES, 1949

W. R. MATTHEWS
K.C.V.O., D.D., D.Lit.
Dean of St. Paul's

GEOFFREY CUMBERLEGE
OXFORD UNIVERSITY PRESS
London   New York   Toronto
1950

Oxford University Press, Amen House, London, E.C.4

GLASGOW   NEW YORK   TORONTO   MELBOURNE   WELLINGTON
BOMBAY   CALCUTTA   MADRAS   CAPE TOWN

Geoffrey Cumberlege, Publisher to the University

Printed in Great Britain by
THE THANET PRESS, MARGATE

PREFACE

THE somewhat magniloquent title of this book will, I hope, be read in conjunction with the sub-title, for I wish to insist that the present work claims to be no more than an essay. When I was invited to give the Maurice Lectures in King's College, London, I found that there was one subject on which I wished to speak, that of the Person of Christ, and that I had certain things to say which had long been occupying my mind. But these reflections were by no means fully rounded out in my own thoughts and seemed to consist very largely of questions which I was persuaded ought to be asked, along with some answers which were tentative and opened out vistas which I had not explored with any completeness. I was rash enough to think that much of the current theology of the Incarnation neglects to face the new situation which Biblical criticism and modern psychology have created. In particular, one might say that the fresh light upon human personality which has come from the psycho-analysts and from psychical research had never been considered sufficiently in its bearing upon the doctrine of the Incarnation. Since I had no final conclusion to commend, it appeared the only course to throw out my ideas in the form of an essay which might be read without undue labour, and I fear that I have made use of the licence of the essayist to suggest thoughts rather than to work them out with rigid consistency.

The first two lectures cover ground which is familiar enough to students of the subject and they will find little that is new in them—except perhaps my errors; they were necessary, however, for the understanding of the problem which is dealt with in the two concluding chapters. A considerable part of the last lecture has been rewritten and expanded so that I hope it is now more intelligible than when originally delivered.

An essay is not expected to abound in references to authorities and public lectures are certainly no occasion for extended quotations. Had I indulged in this scholarly exercise the book would have been twice as long and would have changed its character. Yet there is a risk that obligations to others may seem to be ungraciously forgotten and I take this opportunity of mentioning some to whom I have been indebted. The writings of Rudolf Otto have been much help to me and in connexion with the present subject I have to refer specially to *The Kingdom of God and the Son of Man*. Professor G. S. Duncan's *Jesus, Son of Man* has stimulated my thinking about the relation of Jesus to the Kingdom, nor must I omit the wise and beautifully-written book of Professor D. M. Baillie, *God was in Christ*. Professor S. H. Hooke's masterly *The Kingdom of God in the Experience of Jesus* appeared after these lectures were written, but many years of friendly intercourse with the author have made me familiar with his ideas, to my great advantage, and I doubt not that I have learned from him more than I could easily tell.

Of one thing I am convinced, that the kind of questions I have asked are real questions and that serious thought about them is an urgent need. What in the present intellectual situation can we mean when we say that God was in Christ, and how can we interpret Him and his significance to the modern man? If this essay awakens anyone from 'dogmatic slumbers' to grapple with these problems it will have served some purpose.

W. R. MATTHEWS

London
October, 1949.

CONTENTS

I

THE HISTORICAL JESUS

THE subject which I have chosen for the Maurice Lectures is, it will be admitted, one which would have the approval of the great man in whose honour these lectures were founded, for he was throughout his career deeply concerned with the need to understand Christ and his kingdom and to grapple with the problems which increasing knowledge presents to faith. I shall not pretend that the conclusions which I may suggest are in harmony with his recorded opinions, but I claim that the enquiry itself is one which he would have approved, and I hope that it may be conducted in his spirit of reverence for truth. There is also, I may add, a certain appropriateness in the subject to this place. One of the memories of my past life in this college is that of a lecture given in 1909 by Dr. Sanday which he expanded into his book *Christologies Ancient and Modern*. The theory which he then put forward elicited much criticism at the time and I suppose would not be held by anyone to-day in the precise form in which he stated it, but the book was important, because it attempted to make use of modern knowledge to reach a new and more intelligible conception of the Incarnation. Sanday was impressed by the fresh light on the nature of personality which came from the researches of F. W. Myers and others and tried to base a conception of the divine nature of the Incarnate Lord on the idea of the 'sub-liminal self' which was propounded in Myers's book, *Human Personality and its Survival of Bodily Death.* Much more is now known of the unconscious element in human selfhood and the speculations both of Myers and of Sanday are out of date, but we shall find, I think, that these great men were the pioneers of lines of thought which cannot be ignored by those who seek insight into the nature of man and the nature of the Son of Man.

I

What then do I mean by the Problem of Christ? In the most general terms I mean the challenge of Christ to the intellect—the challenge, not only of the teaching, but of the Person. This is no new thing. From the beginning of the gospel it has come to every age. It was presented first of all explicitly by Jesus himself when he asked, 'But whom do ye say that I am?' The answer was presumably the result of reflection. It was the application of a category already present in the mind of Peter to explain the unique impression which the personality of Jesus made upon him. We shall all agree that the person of Jesus, when once we see him as a real being with the hues of life and not as an abstraction, presents a challenge to us which we ignore at our peril. This is true, I suggest, at every level and phase of our existence. It is most obvious in the realm of personal behaviour and the inner motives which regulate it. 'Thou judgest us, thy purity doth all our lives condemn.' But the challenge extends further, to the societies in which we live and to the very structure of our corporate life. Not less is this true of our emotions and imagination. St. Paul was speaking out of his own experience when he said that every imagination must be brought into obedience to Christ. All this, I suppose, is common ground, but perhaps the challenge of Christ to the intellect is not so generally accepted. I hold that it is a necessary part of our response to Christ that we should seek to understand what he is, to make clear to ourselves his relation with God and man and to relate him with the knowledge of history and of the universe which we, in these last centuries, have acquired. In short, I believe in the need for a rational theology.

There are objectors to the proposition that we can and ought to try to think out the doctrine of the Incarnation. Some would hold, unless I misunderstand Karl Barth, that the Incarnation is 'given'—it is a revealed fact, and the office of reason in theology is, not to dig up the foundations and examine them, but simply to order the data of revelation in a coherent manner. From a very different standpoint, others would urge that the fundamental thinking on the Person of Christ has been done already and once for all. It stands formulated in the dogmas of the Church, which are final and irreformable. The office of reason is to understand them, not to seek a deeper apprehension, or a different one, from that which has been laid down. If, as is indeed the case, the dogmas leave us with a mystery at the end, it is our duty to accept the mystery with adoring obedience.

In each of these views we may discern some truth. No doubt the 'given' is the starting point of any enquiry and, in this case, the given is Christ—the historical Jesus and the creative experience of the Apostolic Church; but for them there would be no problem. But we may still humbly follow Anselm and cherish, not a blind faith, but a faith that enquires—*fides quaerens intellectum*. And no doubt, at the end, we shall still be confronted with mystery. How could it be otherwise? When the self—our own self—is to us, in Augustine's phrase, an 'abyss', how much more the person of Christ! But still there remains the need to say to ourselves, and to others, as intelligibly as we can, what we mean by the Incarnation of the Son. If we are serious in the claim that all true philosophy, and all understanding of history, as well as all true human life, must centre in Christ, we seem to be under the obligation to say as precisely as we can what we mean. It is, at any rate, certain that the Person of Christ, and the claims of Christianity for him, awaken many questions in many minds—some old and some arising out of modern thought —and the mind of man will either pursue them or, in the long run, dismiss the challenge of Christ as unreal.

The problems on which I propose to touch are (a) the evidence of the New Testament; (b) the defects of the classical or orthodox doctrine of the Incarnation; (c) the new situation for Christian doctrine created by modern psychology and philosophy.

As we all remember, the doctrine of the Person of Christ which is summarized in the so-called creeds of Nicaea and Athanasius was the outcome of a long and bitter controversy, which distracted the Church in the third, fourth and fifth centuries. In the course of this struggle the Church evolved the conception of the Christ as one person with two natures, divine and human, being 'of one substance with the Father'. Certain interpretations were branded as heretical and certain lines of thought marked out as legitimate. We shall return to this in the next lecture. Here I want to draw attention to one fact, which is familiar enough to students but sometimes forgotten by the general reader. The Fathers of the great councils based their teaching on Scripture. It is true that they laid stress on 'the tradition', but not as something independent of Scripture. They were not detached philosophers indulging in otiose theosophic speculations. They believed themselves to be defending and safeguarding the truth revealed in the Bible and the faith of Christians from the beginning.

It is generally admitted that the results of modern critical scholarship must have some consequences for theology and there is general agreement that the use of

Old Testament prophecy by the Fathers and by the Reformers cannot be sustained to-day. I find it somewhat surprising, however, that many recent books on the Incarnation assume without argument that no drastic revision of the data of the New Testament is called for. This is surely a short-sighted policy, for our theology cannot be sound unless we have made sure its biblical foundation.

The Christian Church took over, with much of inestimable value, one legacy of more questionable worth from the Jewish Church—belief in the inerrancy, and even in the verbal inspiration, of the Hebrew Scriptures, and this conception of the authority of Scripture was extended to apply to the books of the New Testament when the Canon was formed. Thus the Fathers who formulated the dogma of the Incarnation, together with most of the heretics whom they anathematized, took for granted a view of Scripture which few scholars could accept to-day.

The difference becomes most obvious and acute when we consider the Gospel of St. John. Very much of the argument in the early centuries turned upon the interpretation of texts in the Fourth Gospel. The Prologue to the Gospel, with its momentous assertion that the Word was made flesh, was of course in the forefront, but even more important were certain sayings attributed to Jesus in that Gospel. 'I and the Father are one'; 'He that hath seen me hath seen the Father', were foundation passages for the orthodox, while the saying 'My Father is greater than I' was a constant resort of those who opposed the formula that the Son is co-equal with the Father.

What is the situation with regard to the Gospel of St. John to-day? Certainly the final word has not been spoken on this, the great enigma and the precious treasure of the Church—perhaps it never will be. It would be false to assert that there is any agreement among scholars, when we remember that William Temple apparently accepted, in all essentials, the traditional view of the Gospel, and the last work of Dr. Headlam, on which he was engaged up to his death, was a characteristically positive defence of the Johannine authorship of the Fourth Gospel. It would be an act of impiety on my part, who owe so much to Dr. Headlam's teaching, to dismiss his arguments as unworthy of consideration. There are still eminent authorities who hold that the Gospel of John is a primary historical source for the life and words of Jesus. And yet I must express my clear view that they are advocating a lost cause. There is really no way of reconciling the account which we gather from the Synoptic Gospels with that of St. John. No ingenuity in fitting the incidents together, and no wonderful feats of conjectural harmonization, really meet the case. The trouble lies deeper. We have two irreconcilable pictures of the Central Figure, between which, in the last resort, we shall be compelled to choose. In the Synoptic tradition we have the delineation of one who lived through a genuinely human experience. He had indeed powers denied to other men, but he developed in

2

response to the challenge of circumstance, he was really tempted, he obeyed the will of God not knowing whither it would lead him, he walked by faith and not by clear sight, he knew the agony of despair and of uncertainty of the path he should tread. In spite of some legendary accretions, we can still discern one of whom it could be said that he was 'tempted in all points like as we are' and to whom can be attributed the highest kind of heroism. In St. John's Gospel, on the other hand, what we find is a totally different representation. Though there are echoes of the Synoptic Jesus and he weeps and suffers, yet, on the whole, we have the story of the eternal divine Logos, clothed in flesh, passing through time. He pursues a foreknown way. From the beginning he is the self-conscious Son of God. We need not deny that there are historical elements in the Fourth Gospel, and perhaps in one place at least it makes a well-founded correction of the Synoptic tradition, but it seems to me that we should regard it as primarily a mystical meditation on the Gospel of St. Mark, which employs, particularly in the 'signs', an elaborate symbolism. No: the supreme value of the Fourth Gospel lies elsewhere than in its historical accuracy. It is the primary document for all Christian mysticism and it is the noblest landmark in the course of the development of Christian doctrine.

I do not expect everyone to agree with this view, but I think that critical opinion tends more and more to some such conclusion. In the face of all this, it may be respectfully suggested that theologians who write on the Incarnation are under an obligation to make up their minds what they think about the Fourth Gospel, for if the position I have sketched is sound, then the data which the doctrine must seek to interpret have radically altered.

II

Sooner or later, in any discussion of the Person of Christ we are bound to come up against what used to be called the 'claims' of Jesus. Since some writers object to the word as inappropriate, we may substitute the question, what did Jesus think of himself and his mission? We have seen the difficulty of relying upon the Fourth Gospel for evidence on this matter, and we shall perhaps agree that the root of the difficulty is that the historical facts have been so overlaid by theological and devotional interpretation that we are no longer able to be sure that the thoughts and purposes of Jesus have not been completely obscured.

We turn then to the Synoptic Gospels for this knowlege. We shall, however, be sadly mistaken if we suppose that we have left the problem of data and interpretation behind. The first three Gospels are not detached, objective records. No less than the Gospel of John they are permeated with theology. One of the most certain insights on the Gospels, and one of the most important, is that they are documents of propaganda and edification. The first in order of composition, that of Mark, comes from a circle which was primarily concerned to show that Jesus was the promised Messiah and the Son of God. The theological presuppositions behind the Synoptic Gospels are different from those which dominate the Fourth Gospel, but they are no less obvious. The question forces itself upon us whether these dogmatic conceptions were imported by the authors, who expressed the convictions of the primitive Church, or were in any degree held by Jesus himself.

Here, I suggest, we come upon a real dividing line which separates two classes of New Testament scholars. They divide on the question, 'Do we have in the Synoptic Gospels, in the main, an authentic portrait of the real Jesus, or have imported theological interpretations so distorted the picture that the real man has been lost under the dogmatic vestments?'

As we know, many eminent scholars adopt the second alternative. The names of Loisy, Guignebert, Barnes and Lightfoot readily occur to our minds, but they are only a few representatives of a large school, which, with much difference of detail and emphasis, appears to subscribe to the words with which Professor R. H. Lightfoot concluded his Bampton Lectures: 'It seems, then, that the form of the earthly no less than of the heavenly Christ is for the most part hidden from us. For all the inestimable value of the Gospels, they yield us little more than a whisper of his voice: we trace in them but the outskirts of his ways.'[1]

[1] *History and Interpretation in the Gospels*, p. 225.

But these critics themselves fall into two groups—those who are avowedly not believers in the traditional Christian doctrine of Christ and those who hold still to the substance of that doctrine. The first group offers nothing which need cause astonishment. Though I think they do not succeed in explaining the origin and vitality of the Christian religion, there is no logical obscurity about their position. It is a perfectly intelligible theory that the mythology of divine sonship, of God become man, grew up round the figure of a teacher about whom we can know very little. But I confess that the position of the second group causes me perplexity. We are told, on the one hand, that we can hear in the Gospels only the whisper of Jesus's voice. We are bidden to dismiss as probably legendary the sayings and actions which have been the foundation of the doctrine, and yet we are told that Jesus is rightly called the Son of God and that the Incarnation doctrine of the Church has not been mistaken. There is surely a logical difficulty here. How are we to make the transition from the one proposition to the other? How from so much negation do we pass to so much affirmation? I own that these questions defeat me.

But further, even if we could pass over this difficulty, should we not have made the proposition 'Jesus is the Son of God' meaningless, or at least useless? The core of the doctrine of the Incarnation is not the abstract proposition that God has revealed himself with complete adequacy in some person, but that he has manifested himself in this particular person and that, if we would find God, we must seek him in the words, acts and personality of Jesus of Nazareth. To say then that the doctrine of the Incarnation is true and at the same time that we know practically nothing for certain about the real Jesus of Nazareth is to bring together two contradictory propositions.

We have not quite finished with the so-called 'claims' of Jesus. Does it matter, it may be asked, what he thought about himself and his mission? The doctrine may be true even though we are not able to show that it had any foundation in Jesus's own thought. Now here, I think, the plain man has a right to be heard. I have no authority to speak for that mythical personage, but I suggest that he would feel something like this. He would not suppose that Jesus was in possession of the decisions of the Council of Chalcedon or thought of himself at all in those terms, but he would hold very strongly that the Christian doctrine, if true, must have its origin in the self-consciousness of Jesus. He might be able to conceive that the Son of God should be, when he appeared as a man among men, incognito to all save a few disciples, but he would find it almost impossible to conceive that he should be incognito to himself. The plain man is, I believe, perfectly right; the ultimate ground of the doctrine of the Incarnation must be in the self-consciousness of Jesus.

III

We have seen that the twentieth century has posed the problem of Christ in a new form and I will venture now to indicate where I think we shall find a way towards a reconstruction which will be in harmony with modern scholarship. There is in fact a *via media* which steers between the obstinate defence of traditional views and the scepticism which would, if consistently thought out, destroy the basis of the doctrine of the Incarnation. The solution which I have to propose really starts from an insight of Albert Schweitzer, who insisted in his *Quest of the Historical Jesus* that the Gospels were coloured by dogma, but that the dogma came, not from the authors or the Church, but from Jesus himself.

The first necessary step is to realize that there is a development of thought on the Person of Christ within the New Testament itself. The evolution of Christian doctrine does not begin with the close of the New Testament, rather the New Testament is the record of its first stage. In a general way, we can trace the course of this development from the primitive and relatively simple message of the early speeches in Acts to the elaboration of St. Paul's thoughts in the Epistles—his 'wisdom' which he contrasts with the 'philosophy and vain deceit' of the wisdom of this world. No doubt in formulating what Christ meant to him St. Paul made use of already existing conceptions, such as that of the 'heavenly man', but there is no ground for the suspicion that he was weaving a system of mythology detached from the historical Jesus. The process culminates in the Fourth Gospel, when, as it seems to me, the decisive step is taken of introducing explicitly an idea derived from Greek philosophy and Jesus is identified with the eternal Logos. The question which we have to ask ourselves is not, 'Has there been development?'— that is obvious—but, 'Is the development legitimate?' And by that I mean, 'Has the later teaching a basis in the consciousness of Jesus and is it an explication of what was given there?'

It will be universally agreed that the idea of the Kingdom of God is of primary importance, because it was the burden of the proclamation of Jesus and the framework of all his teaching. Much, therefore, depends on the meaning of this phrase in the thought of Jesus. Misunderstanding has been caused by two mistaken interpretations. It has been held by some that the Kingdom is identical with the Church, and it has been held by others that it is equivalent to the establishment of a secular society based on Christian principles. Though the Kingdom is certainly related in a creative manner both to the Church and to society in general, its effects upon them are indirect and almost, as it were, fortuitous. So far as I can see, the Gospels lend no support to the idea that the Kingdom of God means the progressive realization of social justice inspired by religious idealism. It is natural that we, who, for our sins, are compelled to be thinking always of the future of our civilization, should assume that the Kingdom must be primarily a sociological entity and should look to it for a means of salvation from our dangers and fears, but the Kingdom, as we learn about it from the Gospels, is an exclusively religious idea. It can exist and flourish amid the crash of human societies, for it is concerned with that which lies beyond history. Nothing could be clearer than that the Kingdom, or reign, of God is to be brought in by a gracious act of God himself. We cannot produce it. We can prepare for it. We can even enter it here and now, but it is the act and gift of God.

Though I do not believe that Jesus accepted all the crude notions of Jewish Apocalyptic, but that he gave a profounder interpretation of them, just as he did of prophecy, I cannot escape from the conclusion that the Apocalyptic outlook was very fundamental in his conception of the Kingdom. He looked forward to the coming of the Kingdom in power, a divine event, not perhaps very far off, which would bring this age and all history to a close. This is very important, because it has a direct bearing on the meaning of the title which Jesus accepted as rightly his—the Son of Man. The significance of this has now been clearly recognized, as we may see from the number of studies which have recently appeared, notably Rudolf Otto's *The Kingdom of God and the Son of Man*, and Dr. G. S. Duncan's *Jesus, Son of Man*.

I do not pretend that all difficulties have been cleared up, but I think it may be said that the significance of this title is to be understood by reference to the 'one like unto a son of man' of the book of Daniel and the 'Son of Man' in the book of Enoch. This means that the title Son of Man as applied to Jesus implies far more than that he was a typical or representative human being. It carries a supernatural connotation. He is the agent in the redemptive purpose of God. He represents and acts for God. The Kingdom of God is so closely associated with him that he may be said to bring it with him, and hereafter he will be the central figure in the glorious coming of the Kingdom in power. Thus we can understand why his relation with Jesus determines the position of a man in the Kingdom. It would be untrue to say that, according to the Synoptic Gospels, Jesus preaches himself or makes explicit claims for himself: he preaches the Kingdom, but he *is* the Kingdom, at least in the sense that without him it does not exist.

There is of course much more to be said which we must pass over very briefly. The Son of Man gives the new law of the Kingdom, which fulfils and supersedes the old law. He dies for the Kingdom, taking upon himself the woes which must precede its triumph. The Son-of-Man–Messiah is also the Suffering Servant of God, who bears the stripes of others and, by so doing, heals them.

There have been many persons in history who have believed that they had some divine mission and have cast themselves for a central role in a cosmic drama. Some of them have been men of pure life and heroic character.

The story of the power of fanatical self-confidence is full
of pathos and warning in the sphere of religion. The full
argument which would be required to show that, in the
case of Jesus, we do not have another instance of this
familiar phenomenon cannot be developed here, but we
may observe that the two reasons which appear to have
weighed most with the earliest disciples are powerful still.
Those who have left us the portrait of the Lord Jesus
evidently felt there was no incongruity in supposing that
he had that unique relation with God which was implied
in the title Son of Man. There was a quality in his life and
personality which called forth awe and reverence. In later
times this has been called his sinlessness, and indeed the
absence of any indication of a need for repentence on his
own part in one who preached repentence as the gateway
to the Kingdom is remarkable enough, but the word
does not satisfy us, because it is too negative. The quality
is better described as unbroken filial consciousness, or
perhaps, better still, in Schleiermacher's phrase, 'God-
consciousness', and here we penetrate at last to the root of
the matter, to the reality which gives meaning and life to
the ideas which have clustered round the person of Christ
and which is capable of being expressed in other ideas
perhaps for other times. He could assume the office of
Messiah—Son-of-Man because he was conscious that
always he was one with God and that the life of God lived
in him.

The second reason which weighed with the earliest

disciples was the experience of and faith in the Resurrection. It is a commonplace that without this faith there would have been no Christian religion and no doctrine of the Incarnation. Jesus, as St. Paul says, was marked out as the Son of God by the resurrection from the dead. The situation, I hold, has not changed in essentials to-day. The Resurrection must be the starting point of any doctrine of the Incarnation.

Have we answered the question with which we began? Can we assert that the wonderful affirmations which the Church has made concerning the person of Christ have any basis in the purpose, thought and experience of Jesus himself? If what I have said represents, in the main, the conclusions which a sanely critical study would draw from the documents, I think we can. Jesus believed that he had come to bring all history to a culmination and an end. The Kingdom was the answer of God to the desperate needs of men and he was integral to it. He had, therefore, a unique relation with God, which no other man ever could have, and he was conscious of the unbroken presence of the Father.

The forms in which his consciousness of his mission was mediated to himself and to others had no doubt a certain temporary element in them. The conceptions of Jewish Apocalyptic could not serve as the final and universal formulation of the reality and, when the Church launched out into the world and ceased to be a sect of Judaism, it had to find other ideas in which to enshrine its understanding of Christ. It was forced to be more explicit on the nature of his relation with God and with us.

We are sometimes alarmed by the suggestion that in the original statement of the gospel there are modes of thought which we should regard perhaps as illusory. Particularly, I suppose, this question arises in connexion with the imminence of the end in which Jesus almost certainly believed. It was a part of the Apocalyptic complex of ideas. But illusion simply means that the ideas which were available were imperfect. If we suppose that our modern scientific thought-world is free from illusion, we have totally mistaken the human situation. We see through a glass darkly, and every generation has a different glass. The Son of Man was in the human situation and had the thoughts which were prevalent at the time. That they are not our thoughts does not prove that they were worse. The reality they expressed was in the mind and heart of Jesus and there is ground enough for the faith of the early Church that Jesus is Lord and that God was in Christ.

II

THE
CLASSICAL
THEOLOGY

BEFORE we can consider with profit the impact of modern thought on the doctrine of the Incarnation we must have some clear idea of what that doctrine came to be in the history of the Church. I propose, therefore, in this lecture to treat the well-worn theme of the Catholic doctrine of the Person of Christ with special reference to the influences which helped to determine its form and to the coherence, or lack of coherence, of its substance. I shall refer also briefly to two important attempts in the nineteenth century to restate the doctrine, because I think that they have something to teach us when we approach, in the next lecture, the problem as it is to-day.

The close of the New Testament left several quite fundamental questions concerning Christ without explicit answer. Since it seems to be a law of human nature that all questions which can be asked will, sooner or later, be asked, it was inevitable that there should be reflection on the nature of the Incarnate Lord. What we have in the New Testament as a whole is the valuation of Jesus made in religious experience. This does not mean that there was no thinking going on in the Apostolic Church. There was thought of the most creative kind but it was not systematic. It was intuitive and spontaneous, not theology but revelation, without which theology must wander in the void. Probably we understand the New Testament best when we think of it as the production of men who were seeking for adequate language to express what Jesus meant in their experience, throwing out ideas and words to interpret to others an inexpressible reality. In this way we can comprehend the astonishing wealth and variety of the thoughts which are flung out concerning the Lord Jesus. What a bewildering array of affirmations meets us! He is the Messiah, the Son of Man, the bringer and the centre of the Kingdom of God. He is the appointed Judge of men and, at the same time, the Saviour from the wrath to come. He is the pre-existent Son of God, through whom the worlds were made. He sums up all things in himself. He is the revelation and the proof that God is love and, at the same time, he is the second Adam in whom all are made alive, the inaugurator of a new race of men. He is the express image of the Father and all things consist in him. Or again, he is the great high priest who offers himself as victim in the heavens, and finally, he is the divine thought, or reason, made flesh and dwelling among us. But alongside and parallel with these astonishing affirmations there runs another stream. Never in the most exalted moments of worshipful utterance is it forgotten that all this is said about one who was known as Jesus of Nazareth and was crucified. He was the man who went about doing good, the exemplar of true human life so that we can follow his steps and he is not now, in his exaltation, separate from humanity, for he is called 'the firstborn among many brethren'.

One certainty emerges from all this. From the earliest time the person of Jesus was central in the religion of the Church, though the attribution of divinity to him was not explicitly made at the beginning. Even St. Paul, I think, nowhere definitely equates Jesus Christ with God. The Son is always in his writings subordinate to the Father, and we may doubt whether he would have subscribed to the clause in the Athanasian creed, 'equal to the Father as touching his Godhead'. Perhaps it was not until the Fourth Gospel appeared that the full implications of the common Christian experience were stated. Nevertheless for St. Paul, Christ is plainly on the divine side of reality, if the phrase may be allowed. Through Christ we know God and have our access to the Father.

I have dwelt so long upon what must be familiar to every reader of the Bible, because it seems important to realize that the problem of the Person of Christ and the controversies about it do not arise from isolated passages in the New Testament, but from its whole purport and meaning and ultimately, of course, from the experience which gave rise to it. There is no ground for the naïve suggestion, which we sometimes hear, that by excising a few texts, or explaining them away, we avoid the challenge of Christ to our minds. To do that we should have to explain the whole New Testament away.

I

Of course, the two great questions which present themselves are plain enough. Christianity inherited from the Jews the strict monotheism which it was the glory of the Prophets to have established, and the Church never intentionally compromised that primary affirmation. How then are we to think of the divine Son as rightly to be worshipped and yet to preserve the unity of the Godhead? As we know, the solution, if that is the right word, was found in the end, in the mystery of the Trinity. The second question is more relevant to our present purpose. In its most general form it may be put as follows: How are we to conceive of a person who can be the subject, at one and the same time, of both the series of predicates which we have enumerated? How can one who is truly human, our example, tempted as we are and our brother, be also the Lord, the object of worship, the reason of God made flesh?

The problem was unavoidable and probably nothing but total atrophy of the power of thought could have prevented controversy from breaking out. The issues involved were vital to Christianity and the decisions of the great Councils have been a norm for the thought and devotion of the whole Church. Nevertheless, they had tragic consequences. They marked the beginning of persecution by Christians of their fellow believers. Now was heard for the first time the word 'anathema' pronounced by fathers in God on members of the flock of Christ. Political motives, and even personal rivalries, crept into the discussion of the deepest mysteries of the faith, and, at the end, the Church was left with a series of definitions which were intended as a means of exclusion from the family of God.

The original creed of the Church, it seems, was the simple formula 'Jesus is Lord'. With this watchword the Church achieved the first and decisive expansion of Christianity into the pagan world. In my opinion, that earliest creed should have remained the sole doctrinal test for membership and the greatest misfortune which followed from the Christological disputes was the substitution of the criterion of acceptance of a set of theological propositions, by which to judge a genuine Christian, for that which Jesus himself laid down for his disciples, 'by their fruits ye shall know them'.

I can say this without in the least contradicting what I have maintained above—that the development of doctrine was necessary. The short and simple primitive creed called for explanation. In what sense was Jesus Lord? And on the whole, within the limitations imposed by the intellectual situation at the time, I believe the dogmas were right. What I hold as matter of regret is that they were dogmas—formulas of exclusion—and not doctrines, norms of teaching which the best minds of the church had thought out for the guidance of their brethren.

The development of theology involved the entrance of philosophy into the discussion. Though the Fathers were, as we have seen, convinced that they were interpreting and safeguarding the truth of Scripture and were most reluctant to introduce any non-Biblical language into the statements of doctrine, in the end it was found impossible to exclude the most dangerous of the heresies, that of Arius, without employing a philosophical word, the famous 'homoousios', 'of one substance with the Father.' The philosophy which was available in the Hellenistic world was the later Platonism and we may regard it as one of the providential mercies extended to the Church that, when she had to speak the language of philosophy, there was current a set of concepts which were generally accepted and understood by educated people. We who have to think out our faith amid the present confusion of philosophies, where thinkers scarcely comprehend the meaning of opposed schools and often do not try, can readily appreciate the immense value of agreement on fundamental philosophical conceptions. Unfortunately, however, there were certain serious defects in the philosophy, which affected the doctrine of the Incarnation. The chief defect was the absence of any adequate concept of personality and, since the Christian gospel, in its simplest form, is that the personal God has manifested himself in a personal life, this was bound to be an insuperable barrier to the translation of the Christian message into intellectual terms. As Bishop Barry has remarked in his recent book: 'The Church had to attempt to interpret its experience through the medium of an alien philosophy which, if it were the final truth about things would have meant that this experience was impossible. For it was the limitation of Greek philosophy that it had no true place for personality nor any understanding of it. All this involved the patristic theology in a certain unavoidable confusion of which the results still linger on.'[1]

There was another closely related defect of the Platonic philosophy, which tended to make the problem of the Incarnation take a form which was involved in inevitable contradictions. Aristotle himself had complained that his master Plato had left a chasm between the real, timeless, changeless divine realm of ideal forms and the unreal, changing world of our experience. The criticism was well-founded. I believe that it would be utterly mistaken to deplore the influence of the Platonic philosophy on Christian theology. It was a grace of God that a system of thought so profoundly religious was available, but we may regret the effects of certain elements in Platonism, and this applies particularly to the conception of deity. The essential nature of the divine for those Greek thinkers who believed in it was that it was self-sufficient: being beyond change and having all in itself, it needed nothing and, of course, could neither desire nor suffer. To imagine

[1] *The Recovery of Man*, by F. R. Barry, p. 83.

that such experiences could belong to God was a blasphemy against his perfection. It is obvious enough that such a conception of deity was far removed from that of the Bible. There the essential character of deity is creativeness. The personal Creator works in history, manifests his will in events, does things. Jesus's thought of God is evidently of this kind. His parables, which speak of the seeking love of God, are certainly, at first sight, hard to reconcile with the Greek idea of self-sufficient perfection. For my part, I think that the two concepts of deity remain irreconcilable; however deeply our sight may penetrate and, in spite of all the wonderful subtleties of theologians, the Greek and Hebrew and primitive Christian ideas have never been harmonized. I agree with Bishop Barry that we need a Christian metaphysic which will do justice to the status of personality in existence. Platonism has been called Christianity's 'loving nurse'. The phrase has historical truth, but we do not denigrate the nurse if we suggest that the time has come when the Church might leave her behind, not surely without gratitude and remembering, we will hope, some at least of her teaching.

As we all remember, the final decision of orthodoxy was the doctrine which is technically named the 'hypostatic union'—the union of the two natures, divine and human, in one personal being. But it was found necessary to guard against the possible view that one nature was in any way altered or modified by the union and, therefore, a formidable series of adverbs was added to define the union—

they are to be thought of as united in the person of Christ, unmixed, unchanged, undivided, inseparably.

I shall have some criticisms to make of this theological statement, but before I proceed to that, I will utterly repudiate one objection which is commonly heard. There are still those who, following Gibbon in one of his less admirable moments, deride the whole controversy and the decisions of the Councils as strife about words and a futile making of mysteries. That appears to me to be simply stupid. The Councils were grappling with a real problem and were defending a belief which was really vital to the Christian religion. It was necessary so to understand the God-man that he was not merely a man-God, nor the Incarnation merely an apotheosis. It was necessary to maintain that the Incarnate Christ was really man and really God—both our Lord and our brother. The definitions, whatever their defects, had the merit of negating speculations which would have compromised the essential faith.

G. K. Chesterton has a characteristic passage in *Orthodoxy* in which he represents the catholic faith in its development as a wild and dangerous journey along a narrow path bordered on either side by dark abysses. This is perhaps a somewhat melodramatic representation of the facts, but it is essentially true. Given the doctrine that two natures are united in one person, there is a natural tendency to lighten the paradox by regarding one as fundamental and the other accidental, or to emphasize one at the expense of the other, or again to minimize the difficulty of believing that the union of the two natures covers the whole of the human life of Jesus by supposing that he became divine when childhood was passed. All the heresies, Adoptianism, Arianism, Apollinarianism, Nestorianism, Eutychianism, Monothelitism, are more logical and coherent than the orthodox doctrine. Perhaps it is the chief glory of the Fathers of the Great Councils that they held fast by Revelation and Christian experience when logic failed.

Nevertheless, the doctrine of the two natures in one person, as defined by the Councils, leaves us with so many difficulties that we must regard it, not as a final word, but as a starting point for further reflection. The difficulties, as it seems to me, come to a head in the last controversy—that about the question whether there are two wills in Christ the Lord, or only one. I have noticed that those who, while anxious to be orthodox and priding themselves on it, have not perhaps taken much pains to discover what orthodoxy is, tend, when this question is put to them, to embrace the Monothelite heresy. This is not surprising, for either answer seems to land us in a contradiction. It is vital to maintain the unity of the Person, and it appears to follow from this that there must be a single will. On the other hand, the orthodox doctrine asserts that the two natures are utterly distinct and unmixed and the conception of either the divine or human nature as devoid of will is paradoxical in the extreme and would evacuate the Incarnation, if thought out, of all meaning. Monothelitism then must be wrong. But the conception of two wills in one person which always are in harmony, that is to say always have identical contents, is a conception which many of us will find hard to entertain. The fact is that, in spite of the genuine anxiety of the Fathers to preserve the unity of the Person, they did not succeed in evolving a doctrine which secured this necessary affirmation. Their presentation, carried to its logical conclusion, really issues in the idea of a being who is not a unitary personality at all.

II

We are apt to imagine that most of our religious problems are peculiar to our own time and that no one ever thought of them before. So far is this from being true, that I doubt whether any of the major questions which confront theology to-day has not been debated in previous times. Certainly on the problem of the Incarnation the nineteenth century had much to say and some of it is valuable still. Out of a wealth of speculation I will choose two eminent Christian thinkers, partly because of their influence on the history of doctrine but chiefly because they may help us in our own grappling with the subject.

Friedrich Schleiermacher, who has some claim to be regarded as the first really modern theologian, comes out of the Romantic movement, and the characteristic notes of Romanticism are plainly seen in his doctrine—the revolt against rationalism and the emphasis on experience. This does not mean that there is no hard thinking behind his theology, as anyone who reads his *Glaubenslehre* will have ample reason to agree. Schleiermacher criticizes the two-natures Christology of the orthodox tradition very much on the same grounds as I have suggested and it is interest-ing to notice that he too sees in the doctrine of the two wills the climax of the paradoxes which it involves. He has, however, a more far-reaching objection which is worthy of our attention. He contends that the very use of the word 'nature' to refer to divine being as well as human places the problem of the Incarnation in a false setting from the start, for this language suggests that the Incarna-tion means the coming together of two types of being which are included within the same order or category. The term 'nature' is properly used only of finite things. Thus it is legitimate to speak of 'human nature' in the sense of those qualities which constitute human beings, as distinct from other finite beings, but it is quite improper to speak of divine nature, as if there were a class of divine beings who shared common qualities. This objection goes very deep. If it can be sustained, it implies that the two-natures way of thinking cannot be the expression of the full meaning of the Incarnation—the coming of God into human life.

Whatever we may think of this argument, it illustrates the standpoint of Schleiermacher. In his own view, he does not come to destroy but to fulfil—to find a more adequate formulation of the value-judgement implicit in

Christian experience, or in simpler words what Christ has meant in the religious life of the Church. There is much in Schleiermacher's treatment of this matter which deserves careful consideration. He has the merit of always linking up the work and the person of Christ. There would be no need for a doctrine of Christ's person, but for the fact that we know him, in the experience of the Christian fellowship, as our Redeemer. He insists, too, on the necessary connexion between creation, incarnation and redemption. Christ is the completion and the fulfilment of creation. We must not, however, linger on these topics but proceed to the central idea.

The master-word in Schleiermacher's theology is 'God-consciousness'. He firmly believed that God-consciousness is an original endowment of human beings, no less a necessary element in all human experience than self-consciousness. Of course there are degrees of God-consciousness, just as there are of self-consciousness, and in many men it is dim and confused—in fact it is so in all except the redeemed. On the basis of this God-consciousness Schleiermacher builds his doctrine of the Person of Christ.

The essential idea of Schleiermacher's doctrine can be stated in one sentence—in Jesus Christ the God-consciousness is absolutely powerful. The absolutely powerful God-consciousness *is* the Incarnation for, says Schleiermacher, 'to ascribe to Christ an absolutely powerful God-consciousness and to affirm the existence of God in

him are exactly the same thing'. It is claimed that this way
of approach enables us to conceive without contradiction
that Christ is both God and man. The real humanity of
the Redeemer is secured, because his nature is like that of
all men. He develops as they do and is subjected to the
same influences. The possession of the God-consciousness
does not distinguish him from all other men, for it is
common to them all. In that, too, he is their brother. Nor
again does the sinlessness of Jesus Christ remove him
from the human situation, because sin is not of the essence
of human nature but a disturbance and corruption of it.
Indeed, in the deepest sense, the Redeemer is the only
complete man. In him the creation of man reaches its
fulfilment. The completion of humanity in Christ is also
the point where he is unique; just because he is man
fulfilled he is manifestly divine. In all other men the
God-consciousness is darkened, enfeebled and, at the
best, imperfectly developed. In him it is absolutely powerful and, therefore, he is both perfectly human and divine.

It might seem to follow from this that there are degrees
of incarnation and that Jesus stands, as it were, at the apex
of a series imperfect incarnations. If the God-consciousness is the presence of God, then, one might suppose,
wherever that is found God is, in some measure, incarnate.
I think that Schleiermacher ought logically to have drawn
this conclusion, but in fact he did not. Apart from the
Redeemer, he argues, the God-consciousness is not an
existence of God in us, because it is not pure, it is mixed

with materialistic conceptions and it is not pure activity but partly passivity, while God is pure activity. Only through Christ, through communion with him, can the darkened God-consciousness in us become the revelation of God and the real existence of God in us. In this way, the Redeemer begins a new process of life; he is the completion of the creation of human nature and the starting-point of a new type of humanity. The appearance of the first man constituted the physical life of the race; the appearance of the Second Adam constituted for humanity a new spiritual life, which communicates and develops itself by spiritual fecundation. Perhaps we should not be wrong if we said that, according to Schleiermacher, Christ came not that we might become Christians but that we might become Christs.

A high virtue of German theologians has always been that they draw all the conclusions from their premises and not only those which happen to be convenient, thus saving their critics half their labour. They tell us themselves where the shoe pinches. Schleiermacher deals at length with a question which must present itself to any doctrine of the Incarnation—the moral experience of Christ. How can we admit the reality of temptation and inner conflict in the God-man without implicitly denying the divinity? Or to put the question with the utmost simplicity, How can we claim with any reality that Christ was tempted like ourselves when we claim, at the same time, that his divinity made it impossible that he should succumb? Schleiermacher does not shirk this question. He replies, in spite of the contrary indications of the Gospels, that there could have been no inner conflict. The absolute power of the God-consciousness at every stage of the development of the life of the Redeemer precludes the possibility of division within the self and there could be no motion of the sense-nature, of the impulses associated with the body, which did not become the expression or instrument of the Spirit. The God-consciousness is the determining factor in every act. We must add that this conclusion was probably less difficult for Schleiermacher than it would be for us because he held that St. John's Gospel was the primary source for our knowledge of the historical Jesus.

But the conclusion on moral conflict raises a further question. In what sense then is Jesus rightly described as morally good? Plainly, where the conditions are so different and there is no real conflict of motives, or unruly impulses to be controlled, we cannot use the word 'good' in the same sense as when we speak of a good man. Schleiermacher sees this point clearly and once again draws the logical conclusion from his principles. Jesus is *not* a virtuous man. 'The growth of his personality from earliest childhood was a continuous transition from pure innocence to a spiritual fullness of power which is far removed from anything which we call virtue.'

I do not think that the time we have spent on the theology of Schleiermacher has been wasted. We need not stay to criticize the details of his theory. Questions would have to be raised about the alleged universality of the God-consciousness, which is the foundation of the whole structure. We should have to examine very carefully the proposition that an absolutely powerful God-consciousness is equivalent to the real existence of God in the person who has it. We might perhaps wonder how there can be God-consciousness in the mind of a new-born infant. We might explore the possibility that Schleiermacher has not carefully distinguished between our consciousness of God and God's consciousness of himself. And we have already seen that he is constrained, in a vital respect, to contradict the testimony of the New Testament concerning the earthly life of Christ. All these criticisms and enquiries would be most relevant if we were considering the theology of Schleiermacher as a tenable one to-day, but I suppose no one would adopt his view as a whole. It is hardly a 'live option' as it stands. We shall, however, do well to learn what we can from it.

First, it shows that the kind of philosophical pre-suppositions which are behind the classical dogmas are by no means necessary. Here we have a doctrine of Christ which starts from an entirely different metaphysical position and uses quite other concepts and which is at least worthy to stand beside the traditional 'two natures' formulation and, in my judgement, is in some respects superior and more in harmony with the original revelation. We may be encouraged to think that the effort to speak the truth about Christ in the terms of the thought of our time is not either hopeless or sacrilegious. It would not be too much to claim that Schleiermacher has opened up some of the paths to a new understanding. Foremost I would put the firm setting of our thought in the milieu of Christian experience and, above all, of the experience of redemption. Surely he is right in insisting that the Incarnation must never be discussed as an abstract problem of logic and metaphysics, but always in the light of what Christ is to the experience of the Church. Of course it needs hardly to be noted that Schleiermacher is, in the broad sense, a mystic and his theology springs from an analysis of the mystical life. Here I expect disagreement, but I will express the opinion that we shall more and more find ourselves following this clue in our attempts at theological reconstruction. We may learn something, too, from the failures of Schleiermacher's presentation. The difficulties are often the same as those which haunted the early Church in its theological quest, though in an altered form. We may be warned by this that some at least of the apparently insoluble problems do not spring from a deficiency of the philosophical apparatus but are inherent in the ultimate mystery of God-manhood.

I will refer very briefly to the second type of nineteenth century thought about the Person of Christ—that of the Ritschlian school. I use the word 'school' because the characteristic features of the theology were developed more clearly by some of his followers than by Albrecht Ritschl himself. The note of this school is a deep distrust and dislike of the two elements which were so decisive in Schleiermacher's theology, philosophy and mystical experience. To them the entry of philosophy into theology had involved the paganizing of the gospel. This is the *leit-motif* of Harnack's great history of dogma. But they distrusted philosophy, because they thought that it could not fulfil its promise of establishing on rational grounds a view of Reality. The metaphysical quest was vain, or at least inconclusive. Following Kant, they held that things in themselves are unknowable. Still under the influence of Kant, they emphasized the fundamental importance of value-judgements in religion and, in their extremer moments, appeared at least to be content to dispense in theology with judgements of existence altogether. We are confronted, so we might summarize their teaching, with the Jesus of the Gospels and we see him there as the Lord of the Kingdom of God which, when we consider it, reveals itself to us as the supreme moral good. To speak of Christ as divine, to adopt in practical life the attitude towards him which that statement expresses, is to make a value-judgement with respect to him and one which has no analogy with scientific or metaphysical judgements.

The suspicious attitude which the Ritschlians adopted towards mysticism was connected with their view of the central importance of the historical Jesus. The mystical life and experience is not confined to Christianity; it appears, in much the same guise, in many religions. But the uniqueness of Christianity depends upon the Jesus of the Gospels and we must never regard it as one among the religions of the world, even though we may hold that it is the highest. It is not enough to think of Christianity as the culmination of the religious quest of man. It stands alone and the researches of comparative religion have no bearing upon its interpretation.

The Ritschlian school, like the Stoic philosophy, bears the marks of being made for an emergency. It served a good purpose at the time when the criticism of the New Testament and the advance of scientific materialism under the name of Darwin were causing anxiety in many Christian minds. When the problems of philosophy seemed to be either unanswerable or answerable only in a sense which allowed no place for spirit, it was heartening to be assured that value-judgements were enough, but we may doubt whether the Ritschlians have very much to say to us in the twentieth century. Confronted, as we are, by a great movement which seeks to dominate the world and is founded upon a materialist philosophy which claims finality, we cannot meet it with value-judgements alone. We are compelled to set up the Christian world-view against its great opposite and we cannot shirk the question how the Person of Christ not only fits into that world-view but is its centre.

Yet there is one message from this last Christological doctrine of the nineteenth century which has relevance for us in the twentieth. Though we may not end with value-judgements, we must begin with them. The only starting point for any Christian doctrine is the historical Jesus and his impact upon our spirits and minds. We dare not relinquish that. We are speaking of one who lived and spoke and died and, in the conviction of his followers, rose again, round about the year A.D. 30, and of the consequences of that life in the experience of real men and women from that time until now. We are anchored in history and no flights of metaphysical speculation or mystical religion can be allowed to cut the cable. We must constantly return to the source and submit our theology to its test. The truth that we look for is the truth as it is in Jesus.

III

TOWARDS
A MODERN
CHRISTOLOGY

IN this lecture I have to come to grips with the problem of the Person of Christ as it presents itself to anyone who thinks in the categories and with the presuppositions of the present age. Two preliminary remarks are called for to avoid misunderstanding. We sometimes hear it said that what is vaguely called 'Modernism' exalts the intellectual fashions of the day to a supreme place, as if they were the final word of wisdom. Certainly, if anyone is guilty of that, it is a grievous fault, which I disclaim for myself. I do not doubt that there are many imperfections in our knowledge and understanding and that, in some respects, we have lost hold of truths which were better known in some past generations. My modest suggestion is that, if we are to think at all, we shall have to start from where we are and with the material which is ready to our hand, and moreover, it is only by starting there that we can hope to think out a doctrine which will be intelligible to the educated persons of our day. The second remark is a more personal one. I have no complete and rounded

theory to propound, and I have no ambition to start a new
heresy. My utmost aspiration is to indicate where, as I
think, new ways of thought are suggested by modern
knowledge and speculation and perhaps to give the outline of a view of the Incarnation which, to me at least,
offers the promise of fruitful development.

I

Let us begin with the simplest statement of the gospel of
the Incarnation. The personal God is manifested in
saving power in a personal life; 'God was in Christ reconciling the world to himself'. The concept of 'person' is
plainly central in any doctrine of the Person of Christ and,
as we have seen, the ancient philosophy, which entered so
deeply into Christian theology in the early centuries, was
notably defective in its understanding of the nature of
personality and its place in reality. If there is any aspect
of our problem on which we might expect new light from
modern research, surely it is this. Notoriously there has
been much investigation and reflection on personality and
a wealth of new information and conjecture lies before us.
This does not, of course, mean that the mystery of the
self has been cleared up; on the contrary, it has become
even more profound, but there are new points of view and
new facts, often of a perplexing character, which demand
consideration.

We must touch upon the astonishing development of
psychology in the twentieth century. It is hardly too much

to say that it has transformed our ideas of the nature of the self. Descartes, the father of modern philosophy, when he sought by the method of universal doubt for a certain truth on which to base his thinking, found it, as we all remember, in the fact that he was, in the very act of doubting, thinking, and concluded that he was a *res cogitans*, a thinking substance. The view that man is a thinking or rational being and that reason is the distinctive quality of his nature, is not, I hope, abandoned, but we must admit that it is less self-evident than it once appeared to be. Man is not so rational as he likes to imagine. Nor again is the view that a person is essentially a self-conscious being quite so free from difficulty as was formerly supposed. The unconscious has forced its way into psychology. The hypothesis, which Sanday, prematurely, but surely with foresight, tried to weave into his new Christology, has turned out to be much more far-reaching than he could have conceived. I need not say that the hypothesis raises all kinds of philosophical problems; for example, how can we understand the existence of mind, of psychical events, which are not presented to consciousness? But the hypothesis appears to be so well-grounded and to explain so many phenomena that it must be accepted. We now know that very much of our rational and volitional activity is motivated in the unconscious and that no small part of our reasoning is really a rationalization of obscure impulses from the unplumbed depths below consciousness.

The divisions among psychologists are embarrassing and we must allow for the divergences of eminent authorities on fundamental questions, but one conclusion is evident enough. To say that a person is an embodied self-consciousness, or an organism which is self-conscious, is insufficient. We have to add that the self-consciousness carries with it the unconscious. Consciousness is perhaps only that minute portion of a much larger whole which is illuminated. I cannot help thinking that it is a reproach to modern theology that so little reflection appears to have been given to the bearing of this discovery on the doctrine of the Incarnation. I propose to suggest a few questions which seem to me to need an answer. But before we approach that subject, it is necessary to remind ourselves that there are two different conceptions of the unconscious in the field. The Freudian unconscious has a definitely and exclusively individual reference, and its content is the repressed material of the individual life: it consists very largely of those impulses, desires and memories which are so repugnant to the conscious mind that they emerge into it only in a disguised form, in the symbolism of dreams. Dr. Jung, however, holds that the unconscious has a much wider scope. There is not only an individual unconscious, but a racial one, which interpenetrates the individual unconscious. From this racial unconscious there arise symbols which carry within them some of the past experience of humanity, including the psychological truth which is pictured in the great myths that recur, in varying forms, in so many different periods and historical situations.

It would ill become an amateur to decide where such eminent doctors disagree, but with due reserve and full recognition of the uncertainty of the conclusion, I think the probability is that Dr. Jung has something there, if the Americanism may be pardoned. What precisely Dr. Jung has will no doubt be discussed for a long time, and we may hope that the hypothesis will become clearer, but the general idea explains so much and links on to so many other aspects of personality which are coming into our ken that I feel it cannot be wholly mistaken.

The recognition of the fact of the unconscious raises two fundamental questions with regard to the Person of Christ. The first concerns the 'Libido'. As we all remember, according to the psycho-analytical theory, the older view that man is, on one side of his nature, a bundle of instincts, such as self-preservation, anger, sex, must be replaced by a more unitary conception of his instinctive nature. He is carried forward, as it were, by one subterranean stream, the Libido, which is, in a general and vague sense, sexual and from which is derived the motive force of the personality. Unless I am much mistaken, this concept of the Libido has come to stay, and, if so, we must take account of it in our thought about the Person of Christ. It would help us very much if theologians who write about 'original sin' would consider the relation of the Libido to that doctrine, but, so far as I know, we have very little guidance from them. The orthodox doctrine of the Incarnation held that it was necessary to maintain that the Incarnate Son was born without original sin, therein differing from all other human beings, except, in later Roman dogma, his Mother. As believers in the Incarnation ought we, in the same way, to deny the existence of the Libido in the person of Christ?

We all feel, no doubt, a shrinking from this question, as if we were bringing some wild, untamed and repulsive creature into a calm and sacred place, but our shrinking is the sign that the question cuts very deep. It is, at any rate, one which is patently there, assuming that the Libido is a reality. I do not know the answer to this question. Any possible answer leads to further difficulties. Very tentatively I would suggest that we shall have to hold that the Libido was a reality for Jesus, for the alternative would go far to destroy the belief in the true humanity of the Redeemer. If we deny the Libido in the one instance of Christ, we remove him from what appears to be the essential human experience and could hardly assert with any plausibility that he was really tempted in all points like as we are. Still very tentatively, I would conjecture that the true answer to this question was hinted at by Schleiermacher. He argued that the sensuous material presented to the Redeemer through his physical nature was, at every stage of his development, subordinated to and controlled by, his God-consciousness. We know more about the character of this sensuous material and might prefer another phrase instead of 'God-consciousness', but the main idea is surely right. We have to represent to ourselves the development of a human experience which is, at every stage, triumphant—that is to say that, throughout, the instinctive material, the impulses which well up from the unconscious, are perfectly controlled, harmonized and directed in accordance with the demands of each stage. Impossible as it may be for us to imagine such a development of a personal life, there is nothing, so far as I can see, inherently contradictory or impossible in the conception.

I cannot help feeling that much confusion is caused by the vague and rhetorical manner in which some theologians write about original sin. We are all too familiar with the argument that the doctrine corresponds to facts of human experience, which is undeniable, because otherwise it would not have mantained itself so long as a part of Christian belief, but if it is put forward as anything more than a picturesque way of saying that all human beings tend to fail to fulfil the moral law we need a precise definition of what the doctrine actually affirms. It is meant to be an explanation of one aspect of our experience; not merely a description; and an explanation ought to be explicit. The full doctrine of original sin is, above all else, that every man is involved in the sin of Adam and, therefore, is born guilty and under the wrath of God. The further consequence of this is that his nature has been either completely or very deeply corrupted, so that the image of God has been either wholly defaced or seriously damaged. Though there is a real difference between the Protestant and Catholic doctrines, in principle they make identical assumptions, chiefly that being a son of Adam *ipso facto* involves guilt. The doctrine of original sin does not necessarily imply that the instincts and impulses of the human animal are themselves evil, though of course they may be the occasion of sin (*fomes peccati*). The Thirty-nine Articles remark, somewhat mysteriously, that these impulses 'have the nature of sin', but perhaps we need not consider the possible meanings of this phrase— if any. Evidently the idea that all men could have sinned in Adam is one which cannot be taken in any literal sense, though, as we shall see, there may be a more profound meaning in the phrase 'in Adam' than has been recognized. But our purpose is not to explore or restate the doctrine of original sin but simply to relate the idea of the 'libido' to it.

If it is agreed that the possession of desires, impulses and instinctive drives is not in itself the consequence, or any part of, original sin, then we can hold both that the libido was in the personality of Jesus and that he was free from original sin. We should then have to hold that the Incarnate Lord was exempt from any perversion, enfeeblement or obscuration of the will and reason which is the consequence of original sin in other men; or to approach the subject from another point of view, we might hold that to him was given the full measure of grace to deal with the solicitations of concupiscent nature. If, however, we think that the impulses and instinctive drives are connected with original sin, either as a consequence or as a continuation of the original guilt, then we should have to conclude, either that the libido was absent from the personality of Jesus, or that he was not free from original sin. Either conclusion seems to be full of difficulty —the first psychological and the second theological.

The theory of the racial unconscious opens up a line of thought which may throw some light on an aspect of the Incarnation which offers special perplexities to the modern mind. Both in the New Testament and in traditional theology the Person and work of Christ are represented as having racial significance. Not only, we are told, is he the representative Man; in some way he sums up all things; in the phrase of Irenaeus, he 'recapitulates' humanity. We remember too St. Paul's contrast between the natural and the redeemed man, 'as in Adam all die, even so in Christ shall all be made alive'. These were not meant as metaphorical or poetical expressions; they purport to describe a really existing state of things. The men of the early Christian centuries were familiar with the Platonic realism for which universal ideas were not concepts but substantial realities—more real than the particulars in which they were reflected—and thus expressions of this kind were not specially perplexing, but to us, who have inherited very different theories of knowledge, they are obscure, for we think rather of the individuals

as real and of humanity, or the human race, as an abstraction, a convenient label or general term to cover a class of objects which resemble one another. I do not say that our way of looking at the matter is necessarily right and final, but it is our way of thinking and has been more or less imposed upon us by the scientific method which governs all our thought. If, however, the hypothesis of the racial unconscious is confirmed by psychological investigation, we shall have a strong suggestion, on empirical evidence, that our normal way of thinking about humanity is too individualistic and that our separateness is true only on the level of consciousness while, below that level, we are linked together. Humanity may, after all, be more than an abstract general term. If we all partake in the same racial unconscious, a new meaning lights up the phrase 'in Adam all die'.

But simultaneously a new question presents itself. How then are we to understand the word, 'in Christ'? It must be obvious that modern psychological theories of the unconscious, if accepted, will have a direct bearing on the meaning of redemption. It seems no longer sufficient to say that redemption is through repentance and faith bringing a change of mind and of the direction of the will. All these refer to the conscious mind. But redemption to be complete must embrace the unconscious; a man redeemed only in his conscious self is only half redeemed. The new birth must be effective, too, in the hidden springs of personality. How can this be? How can Christ descend into the underworld of our selves and reconcile us to God there? I do not know the answer, but the question is surely one which theologians must consider. I do not mean to suggest that this radical redemption does not take place. Indeed I think that experience shows the power of the grace of God can transform even the unconscious, but the instances are rare and it may be that one of the lessons which religion has to learn from the new psychology is that it has taken too superficial a view of the meaning of redemption. But still we have the further problem of the racial unconscious. If this is a reality, it is a factor in the personalities of us all. Will any conversion of the individual change the unconscious which he shares with all men? It is hard to see how this could be and probably we have here a question which cannot be answered until we know more about the racial unconscious and its relation with the individual unconscious. At present we do not know precisely what our question means, though it is easy enough to see that it is there.

II

We take the same subject a step further when we turn from psychological analysis to its less reputable but close companion, Psychical Research. I am aware that to mention this branch of study is to arouse prejudice from both sides—from religious and scientific orthodoxy—but I believe that it is foolish not to recognize that Psychical Research may have much to teach us about our mysterious selves. We should not rule out the possibility that the next great advance in our knowledge will come in this part of the field. Eminent philosophers are now aware of the need to take account of the phenomena and their inter-pretation; it seems that theologians cannot long remain indifferent. Let me say at once that I shall not refer to the more spectacular aspect of psychical research, to hauntings, mediums or poltergeists; it will be enough to mention two conclusions which, though still contested, appear to me to be well supported.

The case for telepathy is so strong that one is tempted to say that the only way to retain disbelief in it is by steadily ignoring the evidence. The explanation of this type of phenomenon is, of course, a different matter and there is no agreement, among those who admit the reality of telepathy, on its causation. An hypothesis which does not imply any radical change in our conception of the self might conceivably cover all the facts, but those that have been suggested so far are so complex that it is hard to see how they can be said to explain anything, and those which attempt to account for the phenomena on materialistic lines appear to be out of court. The suggestion that telepathy is due to 'waves' of one knows not what, originating one knows not how, and producing effects which have no relation to waves in anything at all is not illuminating. I think we may say that the phenomena of telepathy tend to give strong support to the conclusion that the absolute separateness of selves is true only at the level of consciousness and that, below that level, there is a linking of selves of such a kind that thoughts, emotions, and even memories, may pass from one mind to another without conscious communication. Of course the nature of the linking remains obscure and any discussion of the possible theories would lead us to metaphysical enquiries which must be reserved for the next chapter. Here it is enough to note that we have important confirmation of the wider conception of personality indicated by modern psychology.

I am bold enough to indulge in a speculation which, if accepted, would have a direct bearing on the Incarnation. Christ, it was said, 'knew what was in man'. This has often been taken to mean that he knew the general constitution of human nature, but perhaps a more personal and detailed knowledge could be supposed which would be more in accordance with the intuitive character of Jesus's mind. We could conceive an experience in which the telepathic content was, so to speak, raised to a vastly higher power than in any known to us. Would that not mean that the thoughts and emotions of many other persons would be present to the consciousness, though neither willed nor voluntarily accepted by it?

But this speculation could be carried much further. There is one aspect of the Incarnation which, though much dwelt upon in the New Testament and in Christian devotion, baffles the understanding. The Incarnate Lord is, as Schleiermacher always insisted, the Redeemer, and we cannot safely separate his Person from his work; he is

what he is because he does what he does and he can do
what he does because he is what he is. Now the redeeming
work of Christ is described in such phrases as, 'He bore
the sins of many', 'the Lord hath laid on him the iniquities
of us all', or in that enigmatic word of St. Paul that he was
made to be sin for us though he knew no sin. The religious
value of these affirmations is beyond question, but they
remain for most believers mysteries which are accepted
in faith without much comprehension of how this could
be. Few, I suppose, to-day would be content to believe
that these phrases mean simply that Christ bore the
penalty for sins which were not his. The modern agonized
grappling with the doctrine of the Atonement bears
witness to the fact that we need some more inward and
spiritual conception of the experience of the sinless Sin-
bearer. It may be that here, coming to us from the dubious
realms of psychical research, we have part of the answer.
Does not some faint gleam of light dawn upon us when we
reflect upon the hidden *rapport* between selves of which
telepathy is one evidence? We could imagine a case where
all the barriers of the self are down and all the thoughts,
emotions and desires of all the world flow in—the muddy
stream of all human mental life. It does not overwhelm the
conscious self, which remains aloof and master of the
inconceivable mass of presented material, but all the
thoughts are present and are part of the total experience.
The conscious self knows them all, not from the outside
but from within, yet in so far as they are evil or foolish,

repudiates them and overcomes them. Would not such an experience be bearing the sins of many and the victory over them?

I pass from this hint at a line of thought which might be further pursued to a brief reference to the second recent development of psychical research—Extra-Sensory Perception. There is a good deal of evidence that some persons possess a curious power of sensing phenomena in the external world not only without the use of the physical senses but in conditions which preclude the operation of telepathy. When Dr. Rhine announced the results of his experiments they were received with natural scepticism, but the investigations of other competent researchers have corroborated the conclusions which he drew. The evidence for the existence of this faculty depends upon an immense number of experiments, generally with cards, in controlled conditions which ensure that the card turned up cannot be known by normal perception by anyone, until the subject of the experiment has given his verdict, and also on the calculation of the probabilities of 'chance hits'. It should be understood that this faculty is not infallible. No subject gets all the answers right, but when the number of right answers exceeds by a large figure the number which could be expected by chance and when this occurs frequently there seems to be a factor which can only be described as some kind of abnormal perception. There is much room still for difference of opinion on the significance of these experiments and even, it appears, on the calculation of probability, so that we shall do well to be cautious in basing any argument upon it, but the evidence is impressive. If this faculty really exists, it raises many difficult questions which we need not discuss here, but we must mention a further and even more surprising manifestation. Competent researchers allege that, in the case of some subjects, the E.S.P. faculty shows itself, not with reference to the card which is actually turned up, but to the card which will be turned up next time or the time after. When it is remembered that under the conditions of the experiment no one on earth could possibly know what the next card or the following one will be, we must own that we are confronted by facts which will not fit into our common ideas of the nature and status in reality of the human mind.

In general the existence of E.S.P. as a human faculty tends to support the view suggested by psychology and by telepathy that the self is, in the unconscious, not confined by the limits which seem to wall in our conscious egos. I do not see that it throws any new light on the nature of the link which binds selves together. But what we may call the proleptic exercise of the faculty, when it perceives that which has not yet happened, opens up a new problem. Shall we not have to reconsider our conception of the relation of the mind to the time process?

Common sense holds that we exist in the present moment and that the past exists for us only in memory and in its present effects, while the future is for us expectation and imagination. This has never been a satisfactory theory and indeed common sense does not hold it consistently, for it has never abandoned the idea of the soul or self as a substance. E.S.P. then, along with other evidence drawn from psychical research, such as clairvoyance, suggests that the common-sense idea is quite inadequate. Empirical observation, quite unbiased by any theological or philosophical doctrines, hints at least that there is an aspect of human personality which is not chained to the present moment and may possibly transcend time. Let us remember this when we deal with the subject on more metaphysical lines in our next chapter.

The more familiar phenomena of inspiration and genius must be mentioned if our picture is not to be intolerably one-sided, though we may deal with them briefly because they have already been more fully studied in relation to our present problem. As we have seen, Myers and Sanday were convinced that in poetical and musical creation which we call vaguely 'inspiration' there is clear evidence of the uprush of the 'subliminal self' and that this is closely connected with prophetic inspiration in the sense that psychologically the two types of experience are analogous. The most striking parallel is the sense of something given which the conscious mind did not fabricate and the feeling of compulsion to express it. In the prophet we have the Word which is not the prophet's word but God's and the necessity laid upon him to proclaim it. In the poet and musician we have the testimony of some of the greatest that their work was revealed to them, that somehow the beauty which they 'created' was not wholly their creation but was there waiting to be embodied in words or sounds. Nor is the feeling of compulsion absent, for the 'inspired' poet is often the servant of his vision and cannot choose but sing. Since Myers and Sanday wrote the psycho-analytical school has enlarged our knowledge of the unconscious, perhaps in a one-sided manner. It has, however, forced upon us the uncomfortable recognition that the unconscious comprises very much which is the opposite of aesthetic or religious value, and for a time it seemed to have the appearance of a sink rather than a fountain of light. The facts which Freudian psychology has revealed, however, do not annul the facts which a study of poetical and artistic inspiration suggest. If we do not understand yet how the two sets of facts can be combined in one theory of the unconscious, that is no reason for denying either of them. Myers's view that the unconscious was both 'a rubbish heap and a gold mine' has at least the merit of recognizing its two aspects, though of course his images are too static to represent the dynamism of the hidden ego. Mr. G. N. M. Tyrell's valuable chapter on Inspiration and Genius in his book *The Personality of Man* is welcome evidence that the significance of the supra-rational experience is once more being understood and not identified with the infra-rational.

The reality of 'inspiration' has obviously an important

bearing on the doctrine of the Incarnation. In the next chapter we shall have something more to say on the subject, but here we will simply note that the Incarnation has always been held to be 'through the operation of the Spirit' and that the interpretation of the Person of Christ as the supreme example of inspiration is not new. Whether it is satisfactory must await further consideration, but one remark of a psychological kind is relevant now. We have to admit the very dubious character of much which comes by inspiration. I wonder whether those who attribute all the great achievements of poetry and art to the Holy Spirit have thought out the implications of this doctrine. No one, I suppose, wishes to deny that the activity of the Holy Spirit is to be seen in creative art or to confine it to the sphere of religion and the Church, but the sweeping assertion that all great literature is inspired by the Holy Spirit could surely only be made by one who had either a very limited acquaintance with literature or a very unusual idea of holiness. The truth is that we have upon our hands a perplexing question. There is literature and art which from the psychological point of view is certainly 'inspired', but which we should hesitate to ascribe to the inspiration of the Holy Spirit. I do not know what the answer to this could be, but we shall do well to remember that not all inspired persons are inspired by God and admire the wisdom of St. Paul when he advised his converts to 'try the spirits whether they be of God'.

This brief survey of some of the new conceptions and

possibilities of human personality suggested by recent psychology and psychical research has, it must be owned, posed more questions than it has answered, but we have perhaps demonstrated that there is important material which needs to be related with our doctrine of the Incarnation. To ask the right questions is the first step towards understanding and we may be sure that changed ideas on the nature of human personality cannot be irrelevant to our thought on the person of the Son of Man. When we take the new knowledge into account we can see that not only do new questions arise but some very old questions take a new form. And the prospect opened up is not confined to an array of fresh problems. There is no ground for supposing that the enlarged conceptions of personality which we owe to modern research will prove to be inconsistent with belief in the Incarnation; on the contrary, they offer new and promising approaches to the central problem. Nevertheless we should be deceiving ourselves if we thought that we can remain content with the psychological method and found our doctrine on its results. Psychology cannot give the final answer to any of the fundamental questions, though it may help us to put them more clearly and indicate fruitful fields for thought. In the end, however, the meaning of personality raises questions which only philosophy can deal with and we must, therefore, be prepared to admit that no doctrine of the Incarnation is possible which does not, implicitly or explicitly, make use of philosophical presuppositions.

IV

TOWARDS
A MODERN
CHRISTOLOGY
(continued)

WE have seen that the well-intentioned attempt to construct a doctrine of the Incarnation without metaphysics is vain. We must reconcile ourselves to the fact that philosophy cannot be excluded from theology. But, as we have already noticed, the present condition of philosophy is one of the chief causes of the difficulty of constructing a modern rational theology. If we could agree with the Scholastic thinkers of the Middle Ages and of the present day that, in all essentials, Aristotle had laid the abiding foundations in logic and metaphysics, we might have an easier task, but if we are not persuaded that this is the case and cannot hold that the history of philosophy since Descartes is the story of the deplorable consequences of a *faux pas*—to borrow William Temple's phrase—we are at a loss for a starting-point. So dire is the contemporary confusion that it is almost impossible to make any statement of a philosophical kind with which all philosophers would agree, nay it is even difficult to make any assertion which all would regard as having meaning. The plight of the theologian who desires to express Christian truth in terms of modern thought is indeed pitiable, but he must do the best he can with the material presented to him by this incoherent age. In the long run, this confusion of minds may be no disaster for Christian doctrine, for it is plainly a challenge and an opportunity to develop for the first time a philosophy from within Christianity itself.

I

In one respect at least the development of modern thought is running in a direction which should encourage us. We saw, in an earlier lecture, that there is an unresolved tension in the classical theology of Christianity between the Hebrew and the Greek ideas of God and that rational theology never succeeded in embracing the God who works in history in its scheme. It is a truism to remark that the tendency of modern thought is to evolve dynamic concepts. We need not enquire into the reasons for this, which are complex, but undoubtedly the influence of science and of the new interest in the meaning of history has been important. One of the consequences of this has been the fading of the idea of 'substance'. The conception of substance has had a long history during which it has assumed many forms and, as we know, it has established itself at the very heart of the doctrine of the Incarnation in the phrase 'of one substance with the

Father'. Not the least of our difficulties in commending the doctrine to the men of to-day is that to most of them the expression has no meaning. For it seems as though the day of this venerable idea is almost finished. Neither in those philosophies which aim at completing the work of science nor in the more speculative idealistic systems is substance a category which is taken for granted. This is a very recent development which would have surprised the fathers of modern thought for whom substance was a self-evident notion. When Descartes concluded his primary meditation with the perception that the one proposition which was beyond doubt was his own existence—*cogito ergo sum*—he interpreted that as meaning that he was a *res cogitans*, a thinking thing or substance. We should now say, I suppose, that all he had a right to conclude was that a thinking was going on. The indubitable fact is not a substance but an activity.

Let us then assume that, up to a point, this more dynamic way of looking at reality is correct. I shall make an important reservation later, but we will see how far we can go with the new view. We must notice that, even when we have abandoned the older ideas of substance and adopted the 'dynamic' conception, we still have to account for certain permanent, or relatively permanent, elements in experience. The old problem of 'universals' is not banished. If reality were merely change or activity, it would be completely unintelligible. It is not so, because we find, or think we find, constants in the flux, or perhaps better, uniformities. Now of course I do not pretend here to give an outline of a modern logic and metaphysics but only to draw attention to some elements in current thought which have a direct bearing on the Incarnation. It is well known that the conceptions of organism and 'pattern' play a central part in much scientific and philosophical thinking. A great constructive writer, A. N. Whitehead, has placed organism as the foundation of his system, but the majority of scientific philosophers prefer the idea of pattern. We need not consider here the difference between the concept of pattern and that of organism for it is evident that they are, to a large extent, the same. An organism is a living pattern. Let us concede then that it is possible to regard the changing world as a complex of moving patterns. I do not claim for a moment that the idea of pattern is entirely clear or that it will carry us all the way, but it is obviously useful. The word is becoming almost a jargon and we hear of 'patterns of behaviour', 'ritual patterns', of the Gestalt Psychology, and it seems that we can regard what used to be called 'laws of nature' as patterns of events. We will see if we can apply the idea to personality.

When Descartes reached his certain starting point, 'I think, therefore I exist', he concluded that he was a thinking being. He was at least partly right. But ought he not to have inferred something more? Did he not perhaps leave out an essential factor? The long meditation which was crowned by the discovery of the *cogito ergo sum* was a feat of will. For hours the attention had been directed towards an end; every disturbing thought or impulse had been checked and, at the moment when the idea became clear, it was held and contemplated by a continuous effort of will. The experience of willing was a part of the experience of doubting. The truth surely is that, though we may hope that man is potentially a rational being, he is now and always a will. Thus from the standpoint of observed development, we should look for the core of personality in the will, including in that term the striving, desiring, conative life which is the matrix out of which the conscious will emerges.

This need not lead to the extreme position of pragmatism or to any theory of knowledge which denies objective truth. The dignity of the intellect is not at stake, because we can easily admit that in its highest exercise, as in the case of Descartes, it may be moved and directed by a pure and disinterested love of truth. We are simply observing that, both in the race and in the individual, the intellect has developed as the servant of desire and will.

Let us attempt then to apply the conception of a moving pattern to the human personality regarded as a phenomenon in the changing world. According to the modern type of empiricism we have to discard the idea of substance as that which 'has' the changing qualities and must think of 'things' as moving patterns of events. The table at which I am writing is a relatively stable and slow moving pattern, while the cloud which I can see from my window is a relatively unstable and fast changing pattern. When, however, we consider selves the position is not exactly the same as when we are thinking of tables or clouds. In order to make use of the concept of pattern we here have to modify the notion of events. The events which constitute a table, so far as I know, have no inner or subjective aspect. The events which constitute persons have two aspects. I know, from my own experience, that the events which are my continuing existence are accompanied by awareness and even that some events happen subjectively. There is good reason to suppose that this is true of other human selves and probably of other animals. Though the events which cause what I call the experience which I have of my friend are of the same kind as the events which cause my experience of a table—they are perceived in the same way—yet unless I assumed that they had their subjective aspect, I should not know my friend and indeed I could not have any friend to know. We are led, therefore, to the conclusion that we need to distinguish two types of event—the purely objective event and that which has a subjective side. We may call the latter 'behaviour events'.

We do not know the exact extension of behaviour events. It may be that some events which we normally class as behaviour events are really not so—i.e., they have no subjective aspect—but it may also be, as Leibniz held, that many, if not all, the events which we normally think of as 'mere' events are really behaviour events. It is at least clear that behaviour events differ according to the degree and quality of the subjectivity which they possess. When we come to the events which constitute personality we find among them a high proportion of those which we describe as acts of conscious will, though of course these are never the only components.

We conceive then that persons are moving patterns of behaviour events—that is of events which have an inner side, desires, motives, choices. Perhaps some support for this way of looking at personality might be found in a familiar but somewhat odd fact: It is generally agreed that personality is a matter of degree. Some selves are more fully persons than others, and it may be that no self is completely a person. This will offer no difficulty in principle to us, because we can attribute this difference to the greater or less coherence and stability of the behaviour-pattern. But it is at first sight curious that the behaviour of the higher and stable kinds of persons is not more predictable than it is. On the whole, we do suppose that the more definitely personal a self is the more certain we can be of the kind of behaviour to expect. An uncoordinated self may act on impulses which appear to have little connexion with those on which it has previously acted. Who would venture to foretell the wayward actions of a child? A formed character is more intelligible and, therefore, its behaviour more predictable. Yet on the other hand, it is the highest types of personality that we hold to be most truly free, and from them come surprising and unanticipated acts of heroism or leadership. The great saints, for example, are those of whom we are most sure at one and the same time that they will not confound us by contradicting themselves in act and that they will do things which we could not have foreseen. The conception of a moving pattern seems to meet this case. We are rightly confident that the pattern will not be shattered, but it is a moving pattern—a pattern of growth—and because the pattern which we see is not our pattern, we cannot tell in detail what it will become. The new acts will be coherent with the pattern so far evolved, but they will not be a mere repetition of the old.

II

We are now prepared for the next step in the argument. We proceed to consider the personal life of Jesus as a moving pattern of behaviour-events, which means primarily of willed actions. I am not maintaining, be it remembered, that the pattern idea gives us a full account of personality—in fact I hold that it does not—and thus I am not putting forward the theory that the Incarnation is nothing more than a certain moving pattern of behaviour-events. I do suggest, however, that whatever else it may be, it is at least that, and I think that this way of representing the case may avoid some problems which have been very troublesome to those who worked with the category of substance.

Now if we wished to put the central problem of the Incarnation in its most abstract form I suppose it would be something like this: How can we conceive that the Universal of universals, God, is fully manifested and present, not in a whole class of individuals but in one individual? In modern empirical philosophy, it seems to me, we have a new conception of universals. The idea that thought can do without universals is chimerical, for without them the phenomena would be unintelligible—a mere flux. The universal in modern philosophy is the pattern of events. In a world which is in perpetual movement and change the permanent and intelligible features are the constancies in the change, the moving patterns which we discern in the ever flowing events.

It is evident that our discussion now requires that we should introduce the idea of the Will of God and raise the question whether the concept of pattern applies to it. Notoriously the Will of God is a subject of great difficulty and many philosophers have rejected the idea except in a mythological sense. The root of the difficulty is that we are unable to represent to ourselves how there can be will in the experience of a Being who is timeless, or whose experience is a '*totum simul*'. We must admit that the divine will is certainly very different in its operation from our wills and that the anthropomorphic picture of the purposes of God which we inevitably form must be totally inadequate, but I do not see how a Christian philosophy could give up the idea altogether, for that would be so deeply at variance with the Biblical revelation that it would undermine the gospel itself. With the caution then that the words we use are necessarily inadequate, we will assume that there is in the divine Experience some element or phase of which our experience of will is a faint but true echo. But if we think of the divine will at all, we must think of it not only as an eternal fact, one act, but as translated into the sphere of time. From the standpoint of time, we must think of the Will of God as a perfectly coherent moving pattern of acts of will, and a pattern which is not yet completed.

Let us reflect a little further on the notion of 'pattern.' Within limits, a pattern can be exemplified on widely different scales and in the most various material. So far as the pattern is concerned, it makes no difference whether it is displayed in the dimensions of the solar system or in microscopic magnitudes. Indeed it used to be said that the structure of the atom was very much that of the solar system, though I do not know if this is now confirmed by recent research. Suppose it to be true, it would illustrate the irrelevance of size and also of the material. It would also illustrate another point about patterns. We should not think it reasonable to say that the atom was a copy of the pattern of the solar system, or the solar system a copy of the atom. They happen to exemplify the same pattern.

I contend then that there is no contradiction or absurdity in holding that the moving pattern of the will of God could be also the moving pattern of the behaviour-events which constitute the temporal and historical aspects of a human life. The scale on which the pattern is manifested makes no essential difference. A personal life of which it could be said that it is of the same pattern as the temporal will of God would be the supreme revelation of God; it would be God manifest 'in the flesh'.

If this is accepted as a possible way of conceiving the Incarnation, a saying attributed to Jesus in the Fourth Gospel would acquire a very definite meaning. 'My meat is to do the will of him that sent me and to finish his work'. That would be something more than a forcible metaphor; it would be an almost exact statement of fact. The pattern of the Father's will, on this hypothesis, is the essential reality of the temporal personality of the Son. It is his life; without it, or departing from it, he would cease to be himself. And the pattern, like the temporal will of God, is a moving pattern—the work is not yet completed.

I put forward this speculation in a tentative way in the belief that it avoids some of the difficulties which arise from the 'substance' theory and with the conviction that it is at least more intelligible to contemporary minds, for many to-day who can make little of the idea of substance are accustomed to work with that of pattern. Obviously there are still problems which we cannot solve and perhaps new ones are suggested by the dynamic conception of 'moving pattern'. I will call attention to one.

We carefully refrained from using language which

would suggest that a personal life is a moving pattern of *conscious* acts of will and of nothing else. Though there cannot be personality where there is no conscious will, the 'pattern' is not composed solely of conscious acts of will. We have said enough in the previous lecture about the importance of the semi-conscious and the unconscious activity of the self and we have shown that these elements must be held to play their part in the life of Jesus. The difficulty which I have in mind is concerned with the will of God. Can it be admitted that the temporal will of God includes within it unconscious or semi-conscious desires and emotions? Probably not. And if not, how can a personal human life be said to exhibit the pattern of the will of God? I do not know the answer to this unless it be that, in some sense, there is a distinction within the will of God which would correspond to the levels of will in human personality. It would be possible to speculate on this, but without much profit, for there can be no means of judging whether our conjectures are on right lines. If anyone is inclined to take the risk, I would suggest that perhaps the divine will which determines the great patterns of events which we call laws of nature might be regarded as the analogue in the divine experience to the semi-conscious will of the human person. But I am inclined to think that we have in this problem an indication that the idea of 'pattern' is insufficient. It serves very well so long as the 'material' of the pattern is homogeneous, that is while we are concerned with 'events' regarded objectively, but when

we introduce two-sided events, and with them the subjective element, we have differences of quality or value
in the events and they cease to be mere units. Thus the
concept of pattern begins to fail us, but that does not
prove that, so far as it goes, it is valueless. A path that
leads us beyond itself may be very useful in a long
journey.

III

But I hope you do not need to be persuaded that we
must go further. Whatever value there may be in the
'moving pattern' conception, it certainly cannot adequa-
tely describe the nature of human personality and still
less the meaning of the Incarnation. Even if we were
satisfied that, in one instance, a personal life showed the
pattern of the divine will, we should still have to ask why,
in this case alone, the pattern was perfect. From the point
of view of the Christian faith we have still to weave into
our theory, if possible, the belief that the Incarnation is a
gracious act of God and that the Son 'came down from
heaven'— from the eternal into time.

Perhaps we have too readily agreed to dismiss the category of 'substance' from our thinking. It is, I believe,
useless and misleading when we are concerned with the
temporal order and with 'things', but it comes back in
another form when we penetrate the inner mystery of
personality. In their timeless aspects persons are sub-
stances—permanent constituents of reality.

The attempt to deal with selfhood as a mere flux or stream of events, or of impressions and ideas, breaks down because the self as experienced is obviously something more than that. We feel and know that we are unique centres of consciousness and activity. We 'have' the ideas and impressions. But when we consider the status in reality of this 'centre' we find ourselves in difficulties. It does not appear to be a part of the events which are presented in its experience and, at the same time, we cannot conceive it as having any existence apart from the experience. There is a paradox about human personality. Man is 'the great amphibian'—on one side a native of the world where change rules everywhere, but on the other side mysteriously beyond it.

Two great traditions converge to assert that there is an eternal aspect of human personality—the philosophical and the mystical. No one could claim that there is a consensus of opinion among philosophers, but it is remarkable that all the great constructive thinkers have, in their different manners, held that there is a supra-temporal basis for the human self: that the 'empirical ego', that which lives through a certain number of years and has some passing experiences, is not the whole self. Spinoza tells us that we know and feel that we are immortal. Kant, though insistent that the self is a part of nature, yet holds that the moral experience leads to the idea of the 'noumenal self' and that the mind which 'makes' nature is itself beyond phenomena. There are many roads which converge towards the same end. To me it seems that the most direct and significant way is by reflecting upon the implications of an act of full self-consciousness. When I know myself, the knower is necessarily distinct from the known, the subject from the object, the 'I' from the 'me'. I can never know the knower in the act of knowing. And yet all that I know, nature, history, other persons, myself, time and space, all exist for me simply as objects of the unknowable subject which is, in some sense, 'I'. Thus I am led to the conviction that there is, at the centre of what I call 'myself', a subject which never can be object and hence never a part of that objective world which comes into being and passes away. In the language of religion, I am body and mind, but also spirit.

As we have seen, some strange developments in psychical research may offer confirmation of this belief, but they are trivial compared with the massive testimony of mystical experience. Those mystics who have essayed to give an account of their inner lives have a wonderfully consistent tale to tell. They come not from one religious environment only but from all the great religions of the world. There are no doubt important differences within the over-all agreement, but they all join in one fundamental affirmation—that there is a divine or supra-temporal centre of the self. There are different names for it—the *nous* of the Platonists, the *atman* of the Indian mystics, the *Grund* of the German—but they all mean, in one respect, the same thing. They mean what Clement of Alexandria meant when he said that, if a man knew himself, he would know God, and Augustine when he said if you would find God, look within. The subject which is never object and the centre beyond time are the commonplaces of the mystics.

We must, however, recognize one deep and decisive difference among mystics and philosophers of a mystical tendency. On the whole, Eastern mysticism has identified the supra-temporal centre of the self directly with the divine—with Brahma or with God, and has regarded individual selfhood as an illusory appearance which the true thinker will leave behind in thought and the truly enlightened contemplative in actual experience. Western mysticism, on the other hand, with some notable exceptions, has refused to make this tempting identification, the '*saltum mortale*' of the self, and has held fast to the ultimate distinction between man and his Creator. The Christian belief about the final blessedness of the just made perfect has expressed itself in the image of the beatific vision, in which the finite spirit has the joy of knowledge and of communion with God but is not abolished or absorbed in Him.

We touch here upon mysteries which no logic or speculation can penetrate. Here we must be content to see 'in a riddle and in a mirror', but perhaps we do not go beyond what is warranted by reason if we conjecture that in the centre of his being, in that knower who is never known, man is in touch with God and even in his most wretched wandering in the wilderness of this world, is always rooted in the eternal being of God. It seems to me that with such a view of personality we could understand the mode of the motions of grace and the inspiration of the Holy Spirit. From beyond, where the transcendental ego is with God, they flow into our temporal lives.

And there probably wisdom would leave the matter, but some remarks seem to be called for on the relevance of this to the doctrine of the Incarnation. It is evident enough that the conception of personality at which we have arrived has some relevance to the Person of Christ and we ought to try to make this more precise. Here we embark upon an enterprise in which we have little guidance, for though the mystical approach to the Incarnation is not new, I am not aware that anyone has thought out its theological implication. Everything we say then must be regarded as in the highest degree tentative, as an exploration rather than a thesis.

It appears to me that we can make no progress in our search without bringing in the difference between the two possible views of the status of the transcendental ego. Since I see no way of reaching a logical conclusion on this question, the only course is to take each view in turn and see to what it would lead. I fear that in either case we shall be left with problems to which I at least have no solution.

Let us first suppose that the timeless subject is ultimately one and the same in all rational beings. From the standpoint of Christian Trinitarianism we should have to interpret this as meaning that the Second Person of the Holy Trinity was the ultimate subject in all persons. This perhaps is not so strange to Christian thought as might be supposed, for the idea that the Logos is the rational element in all creation is a tenet of Christian Platonism and the assertion that the Word is the source of all order and all understanding has no impiety. But of course this would mean, if thought out, that all rational beings are incarnations and that the Incarnation in Christ is the supreme example of a universal truth. This again is not without warrant in the foundation documents of our faith. The Prologue to the Gospel of St. John can be interpreted to mean that the divine Logos lightens every man by dwelling in him. Nicolas Berdyaev's last book *The Divine and the Human*, appears to teach that the Incarnation is a cosmic process (though not of the 'dialectical' kind) in which the humanity of God is realized in time. 'In order to be completely like man it is necessary to be like God. It is necessary to have the divine image in order to have the human image. Man as we know him is to but a small extent human; he is even inhuman. It is not man who is human but God.' (Op. cit. p. 110.) We may perhaps make little of these perplexing words, but when Berdyaev, quoting Augustine, says, quite simply, 'God is more deeply within me than I am myself', we understand the kind of religious experience which is behind the theology. There is a sense in which my own reality is to be found only in God.

Nevertheless the doctrine of the Incarnation which would follow from the conception of the unitary Subject in all personal experience would be full of difficulties. We need not refer here to those of a general philosophical character, though they are formidable enough, but will confine ourselves to those which directly concern the Christian faith. The uniqueness of the Incarnation in Jesus Christ would obviously be imperilled, for we should have to say of every person that he came down from heaven and was incarnate. The difference between the Incarnate Lord and all other persons would be that, in his case, the empirical ego was the perfect expression and vehicle of the Eternal, but we could find no reason in the nature of things why this particular instance should be the only one, nor would it be easy to show that any other perfect incarnation owed anything to the historical Incarnation in Jesus. It is of less moment, but important, that this manner of conceiving personality would hardly escape the heresy of Apollinaris. If the only subject in the God-man is divine, we cannot hold that he is fully human in the plain meaning of the word.

On the whole, therefore, we are led to prefer the pluralistic conception of the metaphysical basis of personality. According to this there are many subjects which transcend our time and space. Though the idea is not without obscurities, we must think of the ultimate subject in each person, not as absolutely timeless, but as created. The finite self in none of its aspects is co-eternal with God nor does it ever cease to be utterly dependent on Him for existence. It has nevertheless a conferred timelessness which distinguishes it from the changing empirical ego. The Incarnation then would be the taking of a created subject by the divine Logos and the intimate union with it so that the human subject, while never ceasing to be human and created, was so intimately joined with the divine that they formed, in the sphere of history, one person. These words are perhaps meaningless and, at the best, they indicate in an abstract way the conjecture which we might venture to make in a matter which is beyond our grasp. We come to a more concrete and comprehensible question when we ask, how could this union of divine and human subjects manifest itself in the life-experience of the God-man?

The phenomenon of inspiration may give us the best clue to the answer. We must own that we do not understand the nature of inspiration, but we have some knowledge of the manner of its operation. The 'inspired' person, whether poet, musician, artist or prophet, has the experience that, intermittently, he is enabled to reach a level of skill, insight, or perception of the will of God which is not possible for him in his normal existence and, when under the influence of the inspiration, he cannot doubt that what he creates, thinks or utters is inevitable and right. The experience may be described either as a sudden enlargement of the self or as the flowing in of some influence from beyond it, though the report of those who have the experience, generally speaking, prefers the metaphor of 'flowing in' from outside, as the word 'inspiration' itself indicates.

We must, however, insist upon the intermittent character of inspiration. Neither the poet nor the prophet is inspired all the time and the experience appears to have very little connexion with conscious effort. The inspired man cannot summon the afflatus when he will. The poets at least are quite explicit on this point. 'Rarely comest thou, spirit of delight.'

> 'We cannot kindle when we will
>   The fire that in the heart resides,
>   The spirit bloweth and is still,
>   In mystery the soul abides;
>   But tasks in hours of insight willed
>   Can be through hours of gloom fulfilled.'

It is the penalty of genius that the fire dies down, leaving its bearer less able to endure the common day, in which normal people live with comparative contentment, and with the dread that it may never be kindled again. The prophetic consciousness seems to have the same quality. The 'word of the Lord' comes in moments of exalted apprehension and the revelation has to be proclaimed and applied by the prophet without the continuous assistance of the invading influence. St. Paul appears to have recognized the difference between those of his utterances which were certainly inspired and those which were not.

What then would a completely inspired person be like? If we take the idea of inspiration to its limit what conception do we obtain? The most obvious answer is that a completely inspired person would be one for whom the power of the indwelling Spirit was always and certainly available. The note of intermittence would disappear. For such a one there would be no vain seeking for inspiration, but whenever his intention and will turned inwards, craving to know the will of God, he would find the response, the insight and the power for the given situation. I suggest that we should think in some such way of the person of Jesus—that is of the Incarnation in its aspect of historical and psychological event. Jesus is the one completely inspired person and, because he is completely inspired, he is the temporal manifestation in a human life of the Eternal Word. In view of what has been said already of the need for a metaphysical basis for the doctrine it is perhaps hardly necessary to state that I am not maintaining that the whole meaning of the Incarnation is to be exhausted under the category of inspiration. We are dealing now, not with the ultimate and eternal ground and significance of the doctrine, but with the person of Christ as a phenomenon in the order of history, and there I maintain that the fact of inspiration is the safest guide we have.

It may be pointed out that this conclusion has ample support in the New Testament. Jesus was hailed as one of the prophets and he was in fact the greatest of them, but he was more than this, because he fulfilled the prophetic movement by living out the prophetic experience to the end. 'The testimony of Jesus is the spirit of prophecy.' The birth of Jesus, according to St. Luke, was 'through the operation of the Spirit'. In the Fourth Gospel the Lord, speaking of his mission says, 'He whom God hath sent speaketh the words of God, for he giveth not the Spirit by measure'. In him the limits which existed in all other inspired persons were absent. The Spirit dwelt in him 'as in no other'.

'As in no other'—that is true in so far as 'measure' is concerned, but it is not true with regard to the manner of the indwelling. Just as in the lower and more limited examples of inspiration the Spirit does not supersede or abolish the human being but raises his capacities to a higher potency, using mind, imagination and will for the divine purpose, so here the fact that Jesus was supremely and immeasurably inspired does not make him inhuman; on the contrary it makes him fully man, the representative man, the human person after God's image. He is at one and the same time truly man and truly divine.

In these lectures I have drawn on branches of knowledge which have not so far been much used in theological writings and I have started some arguments and speculations of which I do not know the conclusion. I do not apologize for this essay, in which I submit thoughts on a subject which sooner or later baffles thought, because I am convinced that reverent temerity of this kind is a need of to-day if Christian thinking is to be vital and progressive. There are some who appear to believe that they show most effectively their faith in the Incarnate Lord by repeating the traditional formulas without attempting to bring them or what they were intended to convey into relation with new knowledge and particularly with new knowledge about human personality. I cannot understand this attitude. Surely if we really believe in the Incarnation, we must hold that it will illuminate all fresh discoveries and in turn be illuminated by them. We should indeed be defeatist if we trembled at every accretion of knowledge as a potential danger to the central affirmation of the Christian faith. We must try to demonstrate that the orthodox doctrine is not an interesting survival of a phase of the past history of thought but a truth which can be stated in terms of contemporary modes of understanding, and further that, when it is thus stated, it can be seen to be a central and co-ordinating truth which, once accepted, brings coherence to a whole range of other truths.

This cannot be done in a moment. The incorporation of fresh insights and the translation of the truth from one idiom to another will be a long and painful process, but it is a necessary and urgent work upon which we ought to enter not with dread but with eager confidence. And we must start thinking now. The conditions perhaps are in many respects unpropitious owing to the confusion of modern thought, but the very incoherence of the contemporary mind and life is the evidence of the need for our effort.

The Christian message has to be reinterpreted and rethought for every age. In our age there are unprecedented obstacles which we must recognize. No single mind, for example, could grasp the constantly growing and changing mass of material which presents itself or estimate the full effect of the transformation of the intellectual situation which marks our era. These lectures pretend to be no more than a modest contribution to a work which must be done by many minds within the Church. If there is anything in them which offends against the deepest reverence and love for the Lord Jesus, may it be forgiven and obliterated, and if there is any glimpse of truth in them, may it commend itself to the judgement of his Church.

INDEX